영어 펜맨십

ABC에서 문장까지...

저자 · Brian Hwang

예성출판사

차례

CONTENTS

- 동시 각운 찾기 ... 39
- 가로 세로 글자 채우기 ... 40
- 알파벳순 문제 ... 41
- 편지 주소 쓰기 ... 42
- 단어 쓰기 연습(1) 신체(ㄱ) ... 43
- 단어 쓰기 연습(2) 신체(ㄴ) ... 44
- 단어 쓰기 연습(3) 야생동물 ... 45
- 단어 쓰기 연습(4) 가축 ... 46
- 단어 쓰기 연습(5) 곤충 ... 47
- 단어 쓰기 연습(6) 새 ... 48
- 단어 쓰기 연습(7) 꽃 ... 49
- 단어 쓰기 연습(8) 채소 ... 50
- 단어 쓰기 연습(9) 과실 ... 51
- 단어 쓰기 연습(10) 운동 ... 52
- 단어 쓰기 연습(11) 나라와 수도(ㄱ) ... 53
- 단어 쓰기 연습(12) 나라와 수도(ㄴ) ... 54
- 단어 쓰기 연습(13) 동의어 ... 55
- 단어 쓰기 연습(14) 반대어 ... 56
- 단어 쓰기 연습(15) 계절 ... 57
- 단어 쓰기 연습(16) 요일 ... 58
- 문장 쓰기 연습(1) 인생 (삶의 정의) ... 59
- 문장 쓰기 연습(2) 인생의 소중한 가치(관) ... 60
- 문장 쓰기 연습(3) 인생의 중요한 가치 덕목 ... 61
- 문장 쓰기 연습(4) 시 ... 62
- 문장 쓰기 연습(5) 기도 ... 63

- 머리말 ... 3
- 일러두기 ... 5
- 알파벳 ... 6
- 알파벳의 종류 ... 7
- 블록체 대문자 쓰기 ... 9
- 블록체 대문자 연습 ... 12
- 블록체 소문자 연습 ... 13
- 알파벳 대문자·소문자 쓰기(블록체) ... 14
- 알파벳 색칠하기 ... 18
- 발음 기호 연습 ... 19
- 블록체 대문자에 따른 단어 ... 20
- 대문자로 시작되는 단어 연습 ... 24
- 그림 속의 알파벳 단어 익히기 ... 26
- 필기체 대문자 연습 ... 28
- 필기체 소문자 연습 ... 29
- 숫자 쓰기 ... 31
- 알파벳 순서 ... 33
- 숨은 단어 찾기 ... 34
- 의성어 ... 35
- 가족 나무 ... 37
- 가족 나무 쓰기 ... 38

머리말 preface

영어는 하나의 학문이며, 학문은 일련의 생각의 체계이자 조직입니다. 이러한 체계와 조직은 일종의 분류이며 자연의 질서입니다. 즉 학문은 교육이며 연구입니다.

교육은 가르침과 배움의 훈련이며, 훈련은 두뇌와 가슴훈련이 되겠습니다. 두뇌훈련은 지식, 전문적 지식과 기술, 논리적 사고인 반면 가슴훈련은 교양, 인격, 성품, 예절, 태도, 감정의 조절, 사랑, 종교 등이라 하겠습니다.

이 책은 영어공부의 머리훈련으로 과학적인 접근(scientific study approach) - '확산적·집중적 학습(extensive & intensive method)' - 과 가슴(정서)훈련으로 적극적 사고방식(positive way of thinking), 즉 '하면 된다('I can do' spirit)'는 정신, '도전과 응전법칙(challenge & response law)'의 지혜를 함양(foster)시키는데 있습니다.

쓰기 란에서는 영어 알파벳쓰기와 읽기훈련은 물론, 기초적이면서 체계적인 어휘력 향상을 위한 집중적인 학습의 요령(knack of study)을 체득(master)하게 됩니다.

예를 들면, 동물; (야생·가축), 곤충, 새, 물고기; 식물, 꽃, 과실, 나무, 채소; 가족나무(나무모양의 가계도); 나라와 수도; 숫자(기수와 서수); 스포츠, 신체부위; 운률(rhyme: 각운·두운), 기도와 시(prayer & poem); 낱말퀴즈(crossword (puzzle)); 반대어, 동의어, 계절, 날짜, 요일, 월별 등을 들 수 있습니다.

바라건대, 세계의 어린이들이 이 책을 통해 영어를 재미있고 쉽게 그리고 보다 체계적으로 공부하여 유익한 활동으로 영어와 전 세계의 문화와 사회를 이해하는데 작은 도움이 되기를 희망합니다.

2010. 9.
in Seoul, Korea

preface

English is a science. A **science** means a **system** or organization of knowledge, experiment or thinking and a **learning**; the former is a classification of things, it's an order of nature; the latter is an education, a kind of study.

Education is teaching & learning and a kind of training brain & heart. Brain training is knowledge, expertise, knowhow, logic thinking, meanwhile heart training shows characters, culture, personality, etiquette, manners, emotion, love and religion, coexistence skill.

This book will foster the pupils of the world by the scientific study. 'I can do' spirit, the law of challenge and response, the wisdom of coexistence.

The penmanship is not only for writing(practice) of English alphabet but also for learning basic English vocabulary, scientific study method- extensive & intensive study.

For example, animal(tame & wild), insect, bird, fish ; plant, flower, fruit, tree, vegetable, family tree-relatives ; nations & capital cities ; numerals-cardinal, ordinal number; sports, ourbody ; rhyme, prayers & poem, pronunciation drill, crossword(puzzle) ; autonym & synonym; season, date, week, months-to kill two birds with one stone.

Writing these words, reading(pronouncing) them, and learning them by heart are a kind of speaking skill, realization of 'knowledge tree', the philosophy of science.

I hope all the children of the world can get learning English with ease and fun through this book, and also this will make them understand English & the world's people, societies as well.

Thanks.
in Seoul, Korea.

 # 일러두기 (Note for explanation)

1. 이 책은 최소한 세 번은 읽고 써야 합니다.
먼저 ○ 표, 다음에 △표, 마지막엔 □표 한 것을 공부합니다.
Read & write this book at least 3 times; first, practice the words with the mark ○; next, with the mark △, and last with the mark □.

2. 먼저 큰 소리로 읽으면서 천천히 씁니다.
At first, read the alphabet or words loudly and then write them slowly.

3. 분류된 단어와 문장은 별도의 연습장에 씁니다.
Write the classified words & sentences on the extra notebook.

4. 학습한 단어들의 점검은 단어를 보고 뜻을, 뜻을 보고 단어를 상기시킵니다.
이때 단어와 뜻 부분을 교대로 가리면서 합니다.
To check for the pupils' understanding at the words and their meanings, the teacher makes sure that the pupils hide the words from their meanings with a square paper or book plate. Then ask the pupils to look at the meanings and speak out the words and vice versa.

5. 날마다 〈발음 연습〉의 단어를 읽고 쓰기를 통해 연습합니다.
머지않아 영어를 잘하는 학생이 될 것입니다.
Everyday read and write the words of special pronunciation practice of B/P, F/V, L/R, S/th(θ). I'm sure in the near future you will be good at English and many friends will envy your English.

6. 약자(abbreviation)
   cf : confer(compare) 비교. 참조하시오.
   pl : plural 복수   sing : singular 단수
   (A) : American(English) 미국식 영어
   (B) : British(English) 영국식 영어
   Q : question(질문) A : answer(대답)

The Alphabet (알파벳)

알파벳(Alphabet) 종류

1) 인쇄체(활자체)

책자를 인쇄할 때 쓰는 글씨체로서 활자체라고도 합니다. 활자의 모양과 굵기에 따라 인쇄체, 필기체 등 여러 가지 서체가 있으나 그 대표적인 것만을 수록하였습니다.

인쇄체	대문자	ABCDEFGHIJKLMNOPQRSTU VWXYZ
	소문자	abcdefghijklmnopqrstu vwxyz
필기체	대문자	𝒜ℬ𝒞𝒟ℰℱ𝒢ℋℐ𝒥𝒦ℒℳ𝒩𝒪𝒫𝒬ℛ𝒮𝒯𝒰 𝒱𝒲𝒳𝒴𝒵
	소문자	abcdefghijklmnopqrstu vwxyz

2) 메뉴스크립트체(manuscript, 블록체)

주로 원고를 쓸 때 쓰기 때문에 원고체(MS) 라고도 합니다.

(1) 대문자 (capital letter) 쓰는 방법

❖ 필순은 알파벳 기본 필순에 따른 것이므로 참고하시기 바랍니다.

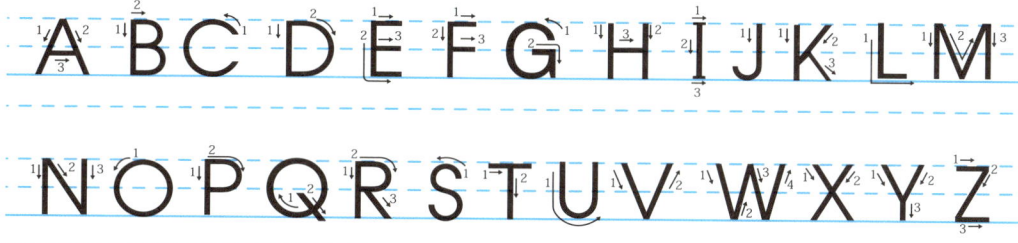

(2) 소문자 (small letter, minuscule) 쓰는 방법

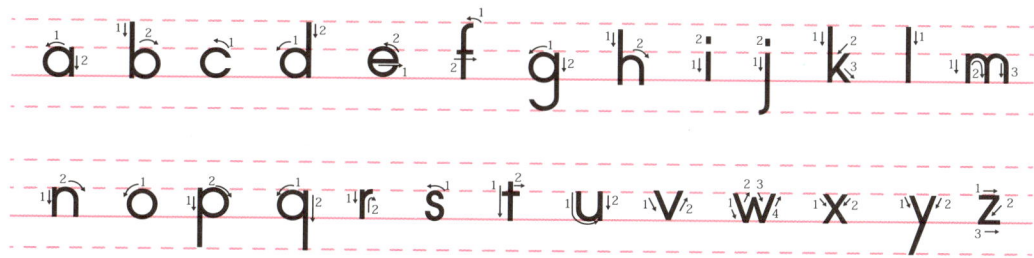

3) 필기체(흘림체)

펜을 떼지 않고 이어서 빠르게 쓰는 글씨체로서 흘림체라고도 합니다. 필기체는 몸을 오른쪽 방향으로 60도 정도 돌린 자세에서 노트 위쪽을 오른쪽으로 25~30도 경사지게 놓고 쓰는 것이 좋습니다. 단, 숫자는 획수가 아니고 쓰는 순서를 나타낸 것입니다.

(1) 대문자 쓰는 방법

(2) 소문자 쓰는 방법

서체 (Calligraphic style)

① 인쇄체 (Print) · 활자체 (Printing type)
② 필기체 (Script) · 흘림체 (Handwriting)
③ 블록체 (Block) · 원고체 (Manuscript)

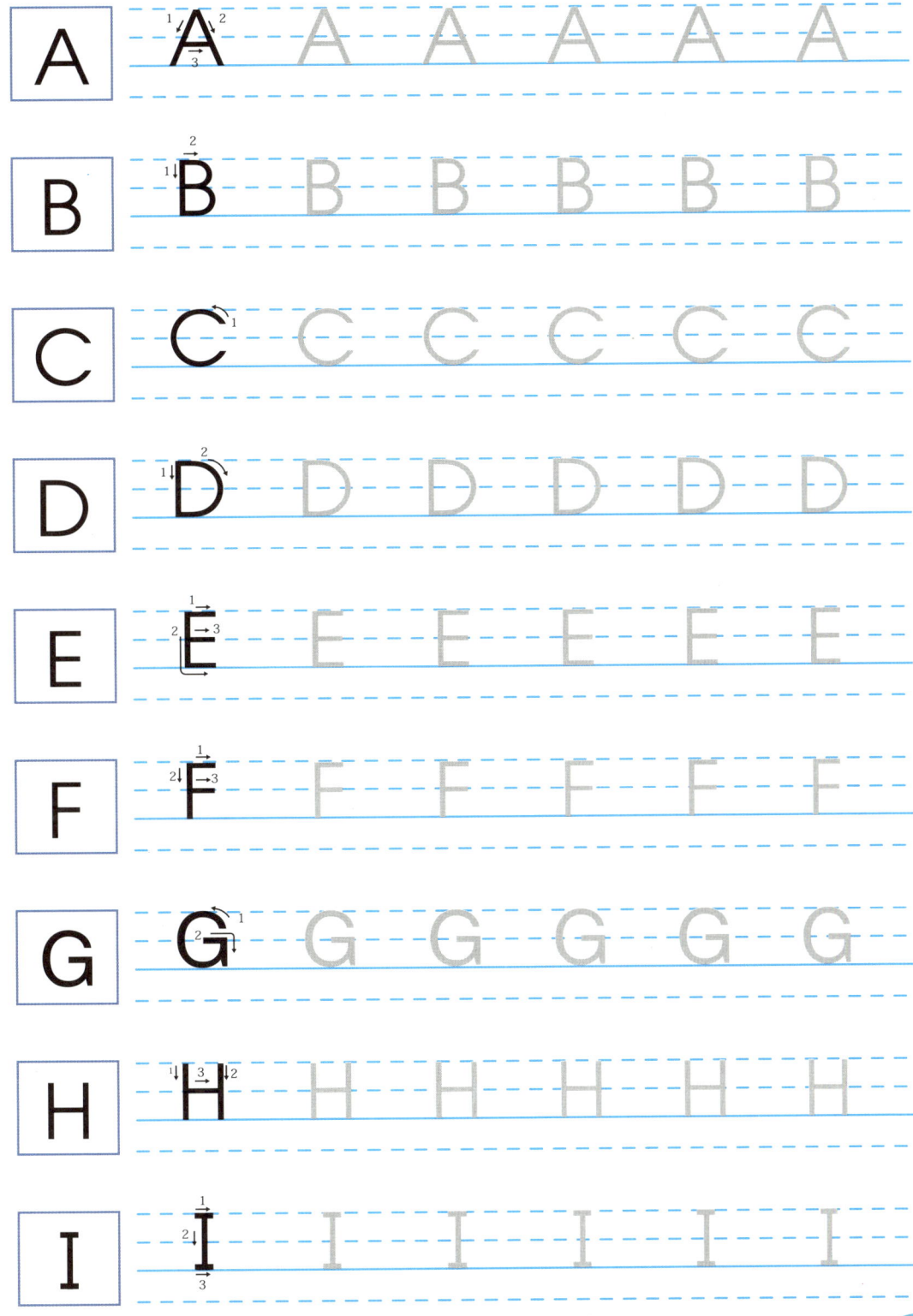

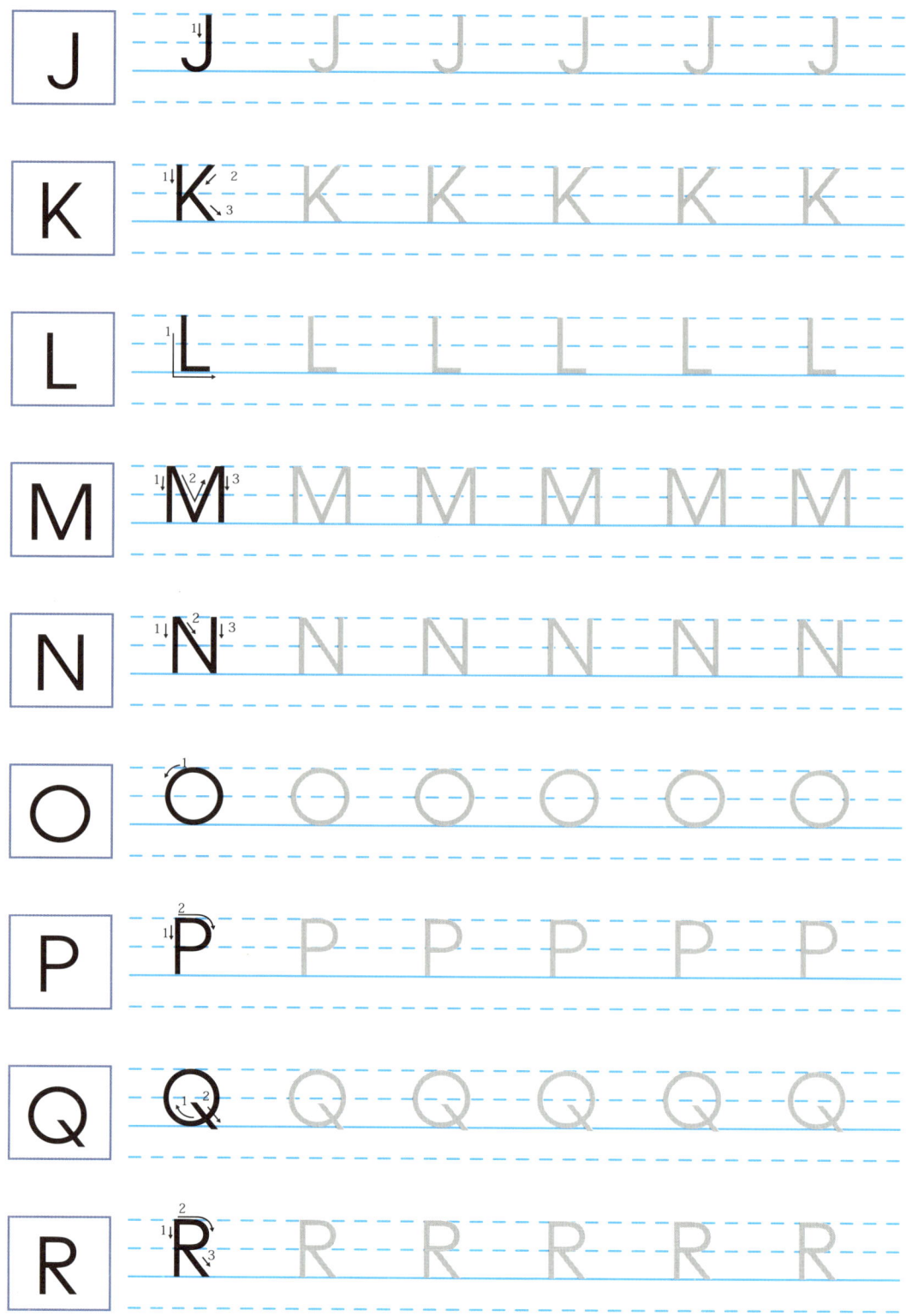

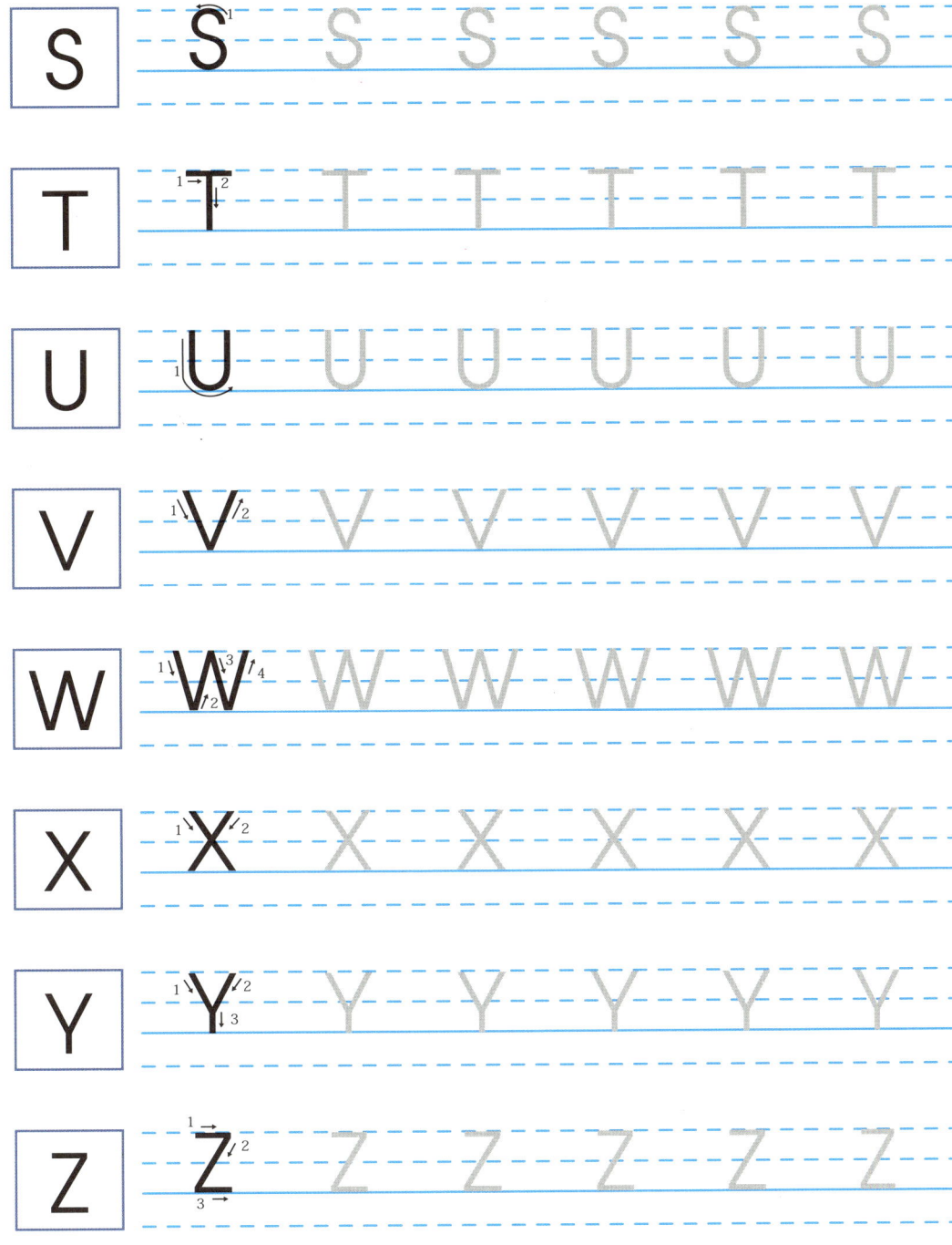

블록체 대문자 연습

A B C D E F G H I J K L M

N O P Q R S T U V W X Y Z

블록체 소문자 연습

a b c d e f g h i j k l m

n o p q r s t u v w x y z

알파벳(Alphabet) 대문자 · 소문자 쓰기 (블록체)

따라 쓰세요.
(Trace and write the letters.)

A a A a

B b B b

C c C c

D d D d

E e E e

F f F f

G g G g

(Trace and write the letters.)

H h H h

I i I i

J j J j

K k K k

L l L l

M m M m

(Trace and write the letters.)

N n N n

O o O o

P p P p

Q q Q q

R r R r

S s S s

T t T t

(Trace and write the letters.)

U u U u

V v V v

W w W w

X x X x

Y y Y y

Z z Z z

알파벳(Alphabet) 색칠하기

알파벳을 순서대로 색칠하면서 소리내어 읽으세요.

발음 기호 연습

아	이	우	에	애	오	오	어	어	아아	이이	우우	오오	아우	에이

a i u e æ o ɔ ə ʌ ɑ: i: u: ɔ: au ei

에어	이어	오이	오우	우어	오어	ㅍ	ㅂ	ㅌ	ㄷ	ㅋ	ㄱ	ㅍ	ㅂ

ɛə iə ɔi ou uə ɔə p b t d k g f v

쓰[ㄸ]	ㄷ	ㅅ	ㅈ	시[슈]	지[지]	ㅎ	치[치]	지[지]	ㄴ	ㅁ	ㅇ	ㄹ(종성)	ㄹ(초성)	우(오)	이(야)

θ ð s z ʃ ʒ h tʃ dʒ n m ŋ l r w j

블록체 대문자에 따른 단어

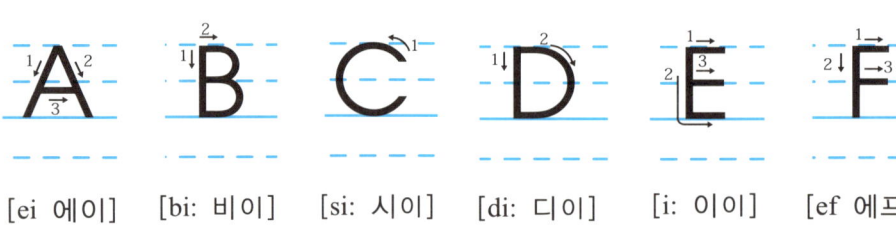

[ei 에이]   [bi: 비이]   [si: 시이]   [di: 디이]   [i: 이이]   [ef 에프]   [dʒi: 지이]

ant [앤트]
A line of angry ants.
성난 개미들의 행렬.

bee [비이]
Buzzing bees.
윙윙거리는 벌.

car [카아]
A racing car.
경주용 차.

dog [도그]
She cuddles a dog.
그녀는 개를 껴안고 있다.

ear [이어]
You hear with your ears.
우리는 귀로 듣는다.

fox [폭스]
The fox family sit on the grass.
여우 가족이 풀밭에 앉아 있다.

gate [게이트]
A squeaky gate.
삐걱거리는 대문.

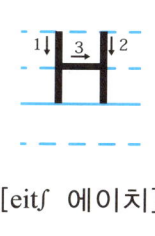 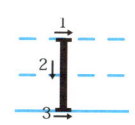   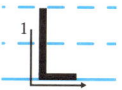  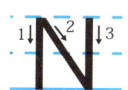

[eitʃ 에이치]   [ai 아이]   [dʒei 제이]   [kei 케이]   [el 엘]   [em 엠]   [en 엔]

house [하우스]
A house for a mouse.
생쥐의 집.

ice [아이스]
It's nice to see mice on the ice.
빙판 위 쥐들을 보는 것은 즐겁다.

jug [저그]
A jug and a mug on a rug.
융단 위의 잔과 주전자.

key [키이]
He kept the key in the ketchup.
그는 케첩(병)안에 열쇠를 보관했다.

lake [레이크]
Can you bake a cake on a lake?
호수에서 케이크를 구울 수 있나요?

map [맵]
Korean peninsular.
한반도.

nut [넛]
A squirrel cracking nuts.
견과류를 깨어먹는 다람쥐.

   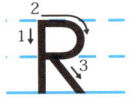  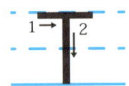 

[ou 오우]　　[pi: 피이]　　[kju: 큐우]　　[ɑ:r 아르]　　[es 에스]　　[ti: 티이]　　[ju: 유우]

oak [오우크]
An oak tree is big and tall.
떡갈나무는 크고 높다.

parret [패럿]
The parrot pecked a carrot.
앵무새가 당근을 쪼아 먹어뗐다.

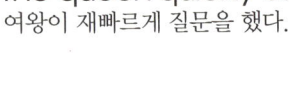

queen [퀴인]
The queen quickly asked a question.
여왕이 재빠르게 질문을 했다.

rabbit [래빗]
A rabbit is nibbling a radish.
토끼가 무를 갉아먹고 있다.

spider [스파이더]
I spied a spider.
거미를 눈여겨 보았다.

tent [텐트]
A bent tent.
구부러진 텐트.

unicorn [유니콘]
A unicorn has a magic horn.
일각수(외뿔말)는 마술적인 뿔을 갖고 있다.

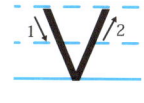 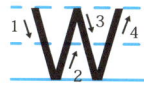  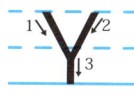 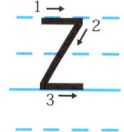

[vi: 브이/비이]　[dʌ́bljù(:) 더블유]　[eks 엑스]　[wai 와이]　[zi:/zed 지이/제트]

vase [베이스]
A vase of various violets.
여러 가지의 바이올렛 꽃이 담긴 화병.

windmill [윈드밀]
A windmill on a hill.
언덕 위에 있는 풍차.

xylophone [자일러폰]
A xylophone makes a ringing tone.
실로폰이 벨소리를 낸다.

yellow [옐로우]
The yellow yolk of an egg.
달걀의 노른자위.

zero [지어로우]
〈Countdown〉 Three, two, one, zero!
초 읽기(최종점검) 셋·둘·하나·영(제로)

대문자로 시작되는 단어 연습

국가, 공휴일, 강, 공원 등의 이름은 대문자로 시작합니다.
(Name of countries, holidays, rivers and parks begin with an upper case letter.)

▸ 나라 이름을 쓰세요. (Write the name.)

United States of America (미합중국)

United States of America

▸ 그림에 맞는 나라 이름을 쓰세요.
(Write the names of the countries under the correct picture.)

America Canada England Korea   (캐나다 / 미국 / 한국 / 영국)

▸ 공휴일의 이름을 쓰세요. (Write the names of the hollidays.)

Memorial Day (현충일)   *Labor Day* (노동절)

Memorial Day   Labor Day

Valentine's Day (발렌타인 데이) *Thanksgiving Day* (추석/추수감사절)
Valentine's Day   Thanksgiving Day

 강, 공원의 이름을 쓰세요.
(Write the names of the rivers and parks.)

Mississippi River (미시시피강)
Mississippi River

Everglades National Park (에버글레이드 국립공원)
Everglades National Park

그림 속의 알파벳 단어 익히기

그림속의 알파벳을 읽고 그에 따른 단어도 읽어보세요.

arrow [애로(우)] 화살

bee [비이] 꿀벌

cup [컵] 잔

dog [도그] 개

elephant [엘리펀트] 코끼리

flag [플랙] 깃발

glasses [글래시즈] 안경

house [하우스] 집

ice cream [아이스크리임] 아이스크림

juice [주우스] 즙

king [킹] 왕, 임금

lion [라이언] 사자

mouth [마우스] 입

notebook [노우트북] 공책

orange [오린지] 오렌지(감귤류)

peanut [피이넛] 땅콩

queen [퀴인] 여왕, 왕비

rocket [로킷] 로켓, 화전

snake [스네이크] 뱀

table [테이블] 식탁

UFO [유우에프오우] 미확인 비행물체

violin [바이얼린] 바이올린

watermelon [워어터멜런] 수박

xylophone [자일러포운] 실로폰

yacht [얏] 요트, 쾌속선

zoo [주우] 동물원

필기체 대문자 연습

$\mathcal{A} \; \mathcal{B} \; \mathcal{C} \; \mathcal{D} \; \mathcal{E} \; \mathcal{F} \; \mathcal{G} \; \mathcal{H} \; \mathcal{I}$

$\mathcal{J} \; \mathcal{K} \; \mathcal{L} \; \mathcal{M} \; \mathcal{N} \; \mathcal{O} \; \mathcal{P} \; \mathcal{Q} \; \mathcal{R}$

$\mathcal{S} \; \mathcal{T} \; \mathcal{U} \; \mathcal{V} \; \mathcal{W} \; \mathcal{X} \; \mathcal{Y} \; \mathcal{Z}$

필기체 소문자 연습

a b c d e f g h i

j k l m n o p q r

s t u v w x y z

a b c d e f g h i
a b c d e f g h i
j k l m n o p q r
j k l m n o p q r
s t u v w x y z
s t u v w x y z

abcdefghijklmnopqrstuvwxyz

abcdefghijklmnopqrstuvwxyz

A B C D E F G H I
J K L M N O P Q R
S T U V W X Y Z

필기체 소문자 연습

숫자(Numeral) 쓰기

기수(Cardinal Number) 로마숫자(Roman Numeral)

1) one _____ (I)
2) two _____ (II)
3) three _____ (III)
4) four _____ (IV)
5) five _____ (V)
6) six _____ (VI)
7) seven _____ (VII)
8) eight _____ (VIII)
9) nine _____ (IX)
10) ten _____ (X)

11) eleven _____
12) twelve _____
13) thirteen _____
14) fourteen _____
15) fifteen _____
16) sixteen _____
17) seventeen _____
18) eighteen _____
19) nineteen _____
20) twenty _____

---

twenty-one, twenty-two, twenty-three, twenty-four, twenty-five, twenty-nine, thirty(30), forty(40), fifty(50), sixty(60), seventy(70), eighty(80), ninety(90), one hundred(100 ; C), five hundred(500 ; D)

---

one thousand(1,000 ; M), ten thousand(1만), one hundred tuousand(10만), one million(100만), ten million(1,000만), one hundred million(1억), one billion(10억)

서수 (Ordinal Number)

1st. fir<u>st</u> _____

2nd. seco<u>nd</u> _____

3rd. thi<u>rd</u> _____

4th. fou<u>rth</u> _____

5th. fif<u>th</u> _____

6th. si<u>xth</u> _____

7th. seven<u>th</u> _____

8th. eigh<u>th</u> _____

9th. nin<u>th</u> _____

10th. ten<u>th</u> _____

11th. elven<u>th</u> _____

12th. twelf<u>th</u> _____

15th. fifteen<u>th</u> _____

19th. nineteen<u>th</u> _____

20th. twentie<u>th</u> _____

21st. twenty fit<u>st</u> _____

22nd. twenty seco<u>nd</u> _____

23th. twenty thi<u>rd</u> _____

25th. twenty fif<u>th</u> _____

29th. twenty nin<u>th</u> _____

30th thirtieth, 40 fortieth, 50th fiftieth
60th sixtieth, 70th seventieth, 80th eightieth
90th ninetieth, 100th one hundredth

101st one hundred and first, 102nd one hundred and second,
103rd one hundred and third
999th nine hundred ninety ninth, 1000th one thousandth

알파벳(Alphabet) 순서

물속의 세계
(Under Water)

아래 단어들을 알파벳순으로 쓰세요.
(Write the word in the alphabetic order.)

① _____
    c _____

② _____
    c _____

③ _____
    j _____

④ _____
    s _____

⑤ _____
    s _____

(조개, 게, 불가사리, 오징어, 해파리)
(starfish, jellyfish, clam, squid(cuttlefish), crab)

숨은 단어 찾기 (word puzzle)

Find out the hidden fruits from the word bank.

H	G	F	E	D	H	C	O	R	N
I	J	K	L	C	M	N	Z	P	A
S	T	V	A	G	R	A	P	E	S
R	L	E	M	O	N	A	Y	R	I
Q	P	P	E	A	R	A	X	S	O
L	M	N	L	G	N	P	W	I	U
H	J	K	O	A	B	P	V	M	C
O	R	A	N	G	E	L	U	M	D
U	O	A	P	E	A	E	T	O	F
A	B	C	H	E	R	R	Y	N	G

[Word Bank]

① corn — 옥수수
② apple — 사과
③ pear — 배
④ orange — 오렌지
⑤ banana — 바나나
⑥ lemon — 레몬
⑦ pea — 완두콩
⑧ peach — 복숭아
⑨ melon — 참외
⑩ grapes — 포도
⑪ persimmon — 감
⑫ cherry — 버찌

(가로, 세로, 대각선 등으로 찾아보세요. 경우에 따라 겹치는 글자도 있습니다.)

의성어 (onomatopoeia)
(cf. 의성어, mimetic word)

고양이 (cat)
야옹 야옹 mew-mew (뮤우 뮤우)
가르랑거리는 소리 purr(퍼어르)

개 (dog)
멍멍 bow-wow (바우 와우)
캥캥 yap-yap (얩얩)

m _____   b _____

쥐 (rat)
찍찍 squeak (스퀴익)

돼지 (pig)
꿀꿀꿀 oink-oink
(오잉크 오잉크)

물고기 (fish)
물고기가 튀어 오르는 소리
펄떡, 철썩 splash (스프래시)

s _____   o _____   s _____

소 (cattle)
음메 moo-moo (무우 무우)

곰 (bear)
우우, 우우 wuff wuff
(우프 우프)

개구리 (frog)
개골개골 croak-croak
(크로우크 크로우크)

m _____   w _____   c _____

꾀꼬리 (nightingale)
꾀꼴꾀꼴 chirp-chirp
(처어프 처어프)

부엉이 (horned owl)
부엉부엉 hoo-hoo (후우 후우)

참새 (sparrow)
짹짹 twitter (트위터)

c

h

t

암탉 (hen)
꼬꼬꼬꼬 cluck cackle
(클러크 캐클)

병아리 (chicken)
삐악삐악 peep peep
(피이프 피이프)

수탉 (cock)
꼬끼오 cook-a-doodle-doo
(쿠커두들두우)

c

p

c

오리 (duck)
꽥꽥 quack-quack (크웩 크웩)

까마귀 (crow)
까악까악 caw-caw (코오 코오)

q

c

가족 나무 (Family Tree, 가계도(家系圖))

가족 나무(Family Tree) 쓰기

1. grandfather _____ [(외) 할아버지]
2. grandmother _____ [(외) 할머니]
3. father _____ [아버지]
4. mother _____ [어머니]
5. dad, daddy _____ [아빠]
6. mom, mommy _____ [엄마]
7. son _____ [아들]
8. daughter _____ [딸]
9. brother _____ [형제, 남동생]
10. sister _____ [자매, 여동생]
11. uncle _____ [백부, 숙부, 아저씨]
12. aunt _____ [(외) 숙모, 큰 (작은) 어머니, 아주머니]
13. cousin _____ [(외) 사촌]
14. niece _____ [조카딸, 질녀]
15. nephew _____ [조카]

동시 각운 찾기

아래시(poem)를 읽고 각운(Rhyme: end rime)을 찾아 밑줄(underline)을 그으세요.
(Read the below poem and underline the words with rhyme.)

Bugs

The bugs ride a bike.
The bugs bake a cake.
The bugs take a hike.
They tun to the lake.

The bugs see the time.
The bugs have a date.
The bugs run home to dine.
They hate to be late.

아래 단어와 같은 라임(rhyme)의 단어를 쓰세요.

bike _____

cake _____

time _____

date _____

벌레(곤충)들이 자전거를 타고 있다. 케이크를 굽고, 하이킹(도보여행)을 하며, 호수쪽으로 향해가고 있다.

벌레들이 시계를 바라본다. 데이트(밀담)를 하다가 식사하러 집으로 뛰어간다. 늦는 것(지각)을 싫어하기에.

가로 세로 글자 채우기 (Cross word puzzle)

빈칸에 들어갈 알맞은 글자를 그림을 보고 써 넣으세요.
(Fill the blank with the suitable letter.)

1.

[고양이, (손)가방, 핸드백]

2.

[팽이, 대걸레]

3.

[(중절)모자, 자동차]

4.

[(깊은)냄비, 단지, 상자]

알파벳순 문제

1. 다음 글자 (letter/ alphabet)의 뒤에 오는 글자를 쓰세요.
   (Write the letter that comes after each of the following letter.)

   (1) f (   )   (2) p (   )   (3) u (   )

   (4) y (   )   (5) e (   )   (6) r (   )

2. 다음 나열된 글자들을 알파벳 순으로 다시 쓰세요.
   (Put the letters in alphabetical order.)

   (1) m k d j (   )   (2) b n l f (   )

   (3) o r p y (   )   (4) t g n s (   )

3. 다음 짝지어진 글자들을 알파벳 순으로 쓰세요.
   (Write the pair letters in the alphabetical order.)

   (1) so su sa se   (   )

   (2) fl fr fi fu   (   )

   (3) dr sl gr pl   (   )

   (4) ri co bu ma   (   )

4. 다음 각 단어들을 알파벳 순으로 다시 쓰세요.
   (Put each group of word, into the alphabetical order.)

   (1) frame fresh friend fruit (   )

   (2) truth try twist tooth (   )

   (3) idea rule pair club (   )

편지 주소 쓰기
(Writing address on the envelope)

대문자로 거리, 도시, 국가의 이름을 쓰는 것을 기억해 두세요.
(Remember that names of streets, cities and states begin with an upper case letter.)

(보내는 사람)

stamp

(받는 사람)

Addresser : 발신인
황 병 찬 (보내는 사람)
서울시 송파구 오륜동
올림픽 선수촌 아파트
321동 301호

Addressee : 수신인
(받는 사람)
Kevin Eisenhut

595-1 Glenfield Road
North Shore
Auckland
Newzealand

From Byeong chan Hwang
      Olympic Village apt. 321 dong 301 ho
      Oryun-dong, Songpa-ku, Seoul,
      Korea

        To Kevin Eisenhut
            #595-1 Glenfield Road
            North shore, Auckland
            Newzealand

자신의 이름, 주소 – 도, 시, 군, 면, 리; 시, 구, 동 아파트 호(수)를 써보세요.
(Write your name, address – do (province), si, kun (county), eup, myeon, ri ; City, ku, dong, apt. (apartment), Room No.)

Name :

Address :

{(동)호수,아파트,동,구,시;번지,리,면,군,(시),도(국가)}

단어 쓰기 연습(Writing Words) (1)

신체(The Body) (ㄱ)

1) arm _____ [팔]

2) back _____ [등]

3) face _____ [얼굴]

4) foot _____ [발]

5) hand _____ [손]

6) head _____ [머리]
   cf. hair

7) knee _____ [무릎]
   cf. lap

8) leg _____ [다리]

9) mouth _____ [입]

10) neck _____ [목]

11) thigh _____ [허벅지]

12) waist _____ [허리]

△ calf (장단지. 종아리 ; 송아지). chin (턱). chest (가슴). cf. breast (유방).
elbow (팔꿈치). shoulder (어깨).

□ armpit (겨드랑이). abdomen (배. 복부). cf. belly. buttocks (엉덩이) cf. hip
forearm (앞팔). upperarm (위팔).

단어 쓰기 연습(Writing Words) (2)

신체(The Body) (ㄴ)

◆ 손 (The Hand)

1) fingernail _____ [손톱]
2) index finger _____ [검지, 인지]
3) little finger _____ [새끼손가락]
4) middle finger _____ [중지]
5) palm _____ [손바닥]
   cf. palm line [손금]
6) ring finger _____ [약지]
7) thumb _____ [엄지]
8) wrist _____ [손목]

◆ 눈 (The Eye)

9) eyebrow _____ [눈썹]
10) eyelashes _____ [속눈썹]
11) eyelid _____ [눈꺼풀]
12) pupil _____ [눈동자]

□ knuckle (손가락 마디). iris (홍채).

단어 쓰기 연습(Writing Words) (3)

야생동물(Wild Animal)

1) antelope _____ [영양]

2) bear _____ [곰]

3) bison _____ [들소]

4) buffalo _____ [물소]

5) cheetah _____ [치타]

6) elephant _____ [코끼리]
   cf. African, Indian elephant

7) giraffe _____ [기린]

8) kangaroo _____ [캥거루]

9) leopard _____ [표범]

10) lion _____ [사자]

11) tiger _____ [호랑이]

12) zebra _____ [얼룩말]

▢ grizzly bear(회색곰), polar bear(북극곰), hippopotamus(하마), monkey(원숭이), orangutan(우랑우탄), panda(판다곰), wolf(늑대).

단어 쓰기 연습(Writing Words) (4)

가축(Cattles, The Animal)

1) cat _____ [고양이]

2) camel _____ [낙타]

3) chicken _____ [닭]
   cf. cock, rooster [수탉]. hen [암탉]

4) cow _____ [젖소]
   cf. bull. ox [황소]

5) dog _____ [개]

6) donkey _____ [당나귀]

7) duck _____ [오리]

8) goat _____ [염소]

9) goose _____ [거위]

10) horse _____ [말]

11) pig _____ [돼지]

12) rabbit _____ [토끼]
    cf. hare [산토끼]

△ drake (숫오리). geese (거위들) (pl). wild goose (기러기).
□ mare (암말). mule (노새). pony (망아지). sheep (양). lamb (새끼양).
  she(he)-cat (암 / 수고양이). she(he)-goat (암 / 숫염소).

단어 쓰기 연습(Writing Words) (5)

곤충(Insect)

1) ant _____ [개미]
   cf. worker. soldier. queen~ [일. 병정. 여왕개미]
2) bee _____ [벌]
   cf. worker. queen~ [일. 왕벌]
3) beetle _____ [딱정벌레]
4) butterfly _____ [나비]
5) cicada _____ [매미]
6) cricket _____ [귀뚜라미]
7) fly _____ [파리]
   cf. dong. horse. house~ [똥. 말(등에). 집파리]
8) dragonfly _____ [개똥벌레, 반딧불이]
9) grasshopper _____ [메뚜기]
10) ladybird _____ [무당벌레]
11) mosquito _____ [모기]
12) moth _____ [나방]

△ bug (빈대. 벌레). cockroach (바퀴벌레). flea (벼룩).
   locust (방아깨비). louse (이).

□ centipede (지네). mantis (사마귀). plant louse (진딧물).
   walking stick (소금쟁이).

단어 쓰기 연습(Writing Words) (6)

새(Birds)

1) crow _____ [까마귀]

2) eagle _____ [독수리]

3) hawk _____ [매]

4) hummingbird _____ [벌새]

5) magpie _____ [까치]

6) ostrich _____ [타조]

7) owl _____ [올빼미]

8) parrot _____ [앵무새]

9) peacock _____ [공작새]
   cf. peahen [암컷]

10) penguin _____ [펭귄]

11) pigeon _____ [비둘기]
    cf. dove [산비둘기]

12) seagull _____ [갈매기]

13) sparrow _____ [참새]

14) stork _____ [황새]
    cf. crane [두루미 ; 기중기]

15) woodpecker _____ [딱따구리]

☐ pelican (펠리컨, 사다새). pheasant (꿩). mandarin duck (원앙새).

단어 쓰기 연습(Writing Words) (7)

꽃(Flower)

1) anemone _____ [아네모네]

2) bellflower _____ [초롱꽃]

3) carnation _____ [카네이션]

4) cockcomb _____ [맨드라미]

5) cosmos _____ [코스모스]

6) daffodil _____ [수선화]

7) daisy _____ [데이지]

8) geranium _____ [제라늄, 양아욱]

9) iris _____ [붓꽃 ; 홍채]

10) lilac _____ [라일락]

11) lily _____ [백합]
    cf. tiger lily [참나리]

12) morning glory _____ [나팔꽃]

13) orchid _____ [난초]

14) peony _____ [작약]

15) rose _____ [장미]

△ lotus (연꽃), pansy (팬지), poppy (양귀비), sage (세이지(샐비어)), sunflower (해바라기), tulip (튤립).

□ chrysanthemum (국화), hydrangea (수국), thistle (엉겅퀴).

단어 쓰기 연습(Writing Words) (8)

채소(vegetable)

1) bean _____ [콩]
   cf. broad, french bean [잠두, 강낭콩]
2) beet _____ [비트, 근대 ; 사탕무]
3) cabbage _____ [양배추]
   cf. chinese cabbage [배추]
4) carrot _____ [당근]
5) corn _____ [옥수수]
6) cucumber _____ [오이]
7) eggplant _____ [가지]
8) garlic _____ [마늘]
9) lettuce _____ [양상추]
10) mushroom _____ [버섯]
11) onion _____ [양파]
    cf. spring onion [실파]
12) pea _____ [완두콩]
    cf. peanut [땅콩] green pea

△ broccoli(브로콜리), celery(셀러리), red pepper(고추), paprika(파프리카), potato(감자), sweet potato(고구마), pumpkin(호박), spinach(시금치), tomato(토마토),

□ asparagus(아스파라거스), lotus root(연근), spanish paprika(피망), radish(무), turnip(순무),

단어 쓰기 연습(Writing Words) (9)

과실(Fruit)

1) apple _____ [사과]

2) apricot _____ [살구]

3) banana _____ [바나나]

4) cherry _____ [버찌. 체리]

5) chestnut _____ [밤]

6) date _____ [대추]

7) grape _____ [포도]
   cf. grapefruit(자몽). raisin (건포도)

8) kiwi fruit _____ [키위프루트. 양다래]

9) lemon _____ [레몬]

10) melon _____ [참외]
    cf. watermelon(수박)

11) orange _____ [오렌지. 귤]

12) peach _____ [복숭아]

13) pear _____ [배]

14) plum _____ [자두. 오얏]

15) strawberry _____ [딸기]

△ coconut(코코넛). lime(라임). mango(망고). papaya(파파야).
  pineapple(파인애플). walnut(호두). almond(아몬드).

□ avocado(아보카도). hazelnut(개암열매).
  persimmon(감). pomegranate(석류). tangerine(탄제린).

단어 쓰기 연습(Writing Words) (10)

운동(Sports)

1) baseball _____ [야구]
   cf. softball [소프트볼]

2) basketball _____ [농구]
   cf. netball [영국. 호주. 뉴질랜드]

3) football _____ [축구]
   cf. soccer

4) golf _____ [골프]

5) handball _____ [송구. 핸드볼]

6) horse riding _____ [승마]

7) marathon _____ [마라톤]
   cf. 42.195km

8) ping pong _____ [탁구]
   cf. table tennis

9) skationg _____ [스케이팅]
   cf. figure. speed skating

10) swimming _____ [수영]
    cf. backstroke. butterfly. freestyle ; diving [다이빙]

11) tennis _____ [정구]

12) wrestling _____ [씨름. 레슬링]

△ cricket(크리켓; 귀뚜라미). hockey(하키). ice(field) hockey(아이스 하키). boxing(권투). bowling(볼링). fencing(펜싱. 검술). shooting(사격). skiing(스키).

□ American football(미식축구. 럭비). rugby football. gymnastics(체조경기). field athlete(육상)cf. field and track. squash(스쿼시)cf. racquetball.

단어 쓰기 연습(Writing Words) (11)

나라와 수도(Countries and Capital Cities) (ㄱ)

1) Algeria (Algiers) _____ [알제리아]

2) Austria (Vienna) _____ [오스트리아]

3) Australia (Canberra) _____ [오스트레일리아]

4) Brazil (Brasilia) _____ [브라질]

5) Canada (Ottawa) _____ [캐나다]

6) Colombia (Bogota) _____ [콜롬비아]

7) Denmark (Copenhagen) _____ [덴마크]

8) Egypt (Cairo) _____ [이집트]

9) Finland (Helsinki) _____ [필란드]

10) Germany (Berlin) _____ [독일. 저머니]

11) India (New Delhi) _____ [인도. 인디아]

12) Italy (Rome) _____ [이탈리아. 이태리]

단어 쓰기 연습(Writing Words) (12)

나라와 수도(Countries and Capital Cities) (ㄴ)

1) South Korea (Seoul) _____ [한국. 코리아]

2) Mexico (Mexico City) _____ [멕시코]

3) Mongolia (Ulan Bator) _____ [몽골]

4) Nepal (Kathmandu) _____ [네팔]

5) Nigeria (Abunja) _____ [나이지리아]

6) Peru (Lima) _____ [페루]

7) Philippines (Manila) _____ [필리핀]

8) Republic of South Africa (Cape Town) _____ [남아공화국. 남아프리카]

9) Saudi Arabia (Riyadh) _____ [사우디아라비아]

10) Taiwan (Taipei)
    cf. Formosa _____ [대만. 타이완]

11) Vietnam (Hanoi) _____ [베트남]

12) Zimbabwe (Harare) _____ [짐바브웨]

단어 쓰기 연습(Writing Words) (13)

동의어 (Synonym)

1) ask　　　＿＿＿＿＿＿＿ question ＿＿＿＿＿＿＿　　[묻다]

2) begin　　＿＿＿＿＿＿＿ start ＿＿＿＿＿＿＿　　[시작하다]

3) change　＿＿＿＿＿＿＿ alter ＿＿＿＿＿＿＿　　[변화. 바꾸다]

4) choose　＿＿＿＿＿＿＿ select ＿＿＿＿＿＿＿　　[선택하다. 고르다]

5) have　　＿＿＿＿＿＿＿ own ＿＿＿＿＿＿＿　　[가지다]
　　　　　　　　　　　cf. possess

6) bad　　　＿＿＿＿＿＿＿ wrong ＿＿＿＿＿＿＿　　[나쁜]

7) difficult　＿＿＿＿＿＿＿ hard ＿＿＿＿＿＿＿　　[어려운]

8) foolish　＿＿＿＿＿＿＿ silly ＿＿＿＿＿＿＿　　[어리석은]
　　　　　　　　　　　cf. stupid

9) funny　　＿＿＿＿＿＿＿ interesting ＿＿＿＿＿＿＿　　[재미있는]

10) help　　＿＿＿＿＿＿＿ aid ＿＿＿＿＿＿＿　　[도움. 원조]

11) present　＿＿＿＿＿＿＿ gift ＿＿＿＿＿＿＿　　[선물]

12) shop　　＿＿＿＿＿＿＿ store ＿＿＿＿＿＿＿　　[가게]

단어 쓰기 연습(Writing Words) (14)

반대어(Antonym. Opposite)

1) big _____ small _____ [큰 / 작은]

2) clean _____ dirty _____ [깨끗한 / 더러운]

3) cold _____ hot _____ [추운 / 더운]

4) difficult _____ easy _____ [어려운 / 쉬운]
   cf. hard

5) fast _____ slow _____ [빠른 / 느린]
   cf. rapid

6) good _____ bad _____ [좋은 / 나쁜]

7) high _____ low _____ [높은 / 낮은]

8) light _____ heavy _____ [가벼운; 밝은 / 무거운]
                      cf. dark (어두운)

9) long _____ short _____ [긴 / 짧은]

10) old _____ new _____ [오래된; 늙은 / 새로운]
                     cf. young (젊은)

11) tall _____ short _____ [키큰 / 키 작은]

12) warm _____ cool _____ [따뜻한 / 서늘한]
                      cf. chill (쌀쌀한. 냉기)

단어 쓰기 연습(Writing Words) (15)

계절(Season)

Q. What season do you like best?
어떤 (무슨)계절을 제일 좋아하니?

Which season do you like better, spring or autumn?
봄 · 가을 중 어느 계절이 더 좋으니?

A. I like summer(winter) best.
여름(겨울)을 가장 좋아해.

I like spring(fall) better.
봄(가을)을 더 좋아해.

Q. What are six seasons? (Riddle)
여섯 계절 (양념)은 (어떤 것들이지?) 무엇이지?

A. They are spring, summer, fall, winter and salt and pepper.
봄, 여름, 가을, 겨울, 그리고 소금과 후추(가루)야.

1) spring _____ [봄]

2) summer _____ [여름]

3) autumn _____ [가을]
   cf. fall(가을. 폭포. 떨어지다. 넘어지다)

4) winter _____ [겨울]

5) salt _____ [소금]
   cf. salary (봉급. 급여)

6) pepper _____ [후추. 고추]
   cf. black, white~ (후춧가루) red~ (고추)

7) season _____ [계절. 절기 ; 양념(하다)]
   cf. seasoning (양념하기. 조미료. 길들이기)

단어 쓰기 연습(Writing Words) (16)

요일(Week (day))

Q. What day is it today?   오늘 무슨 요일이야?
A. It's Monday.   월요일이야.
Q. What date is it today?   오늘 며칠이지?
A. It's May 5. (5th of May).   5월 5일이야.

1) Sunday _____ [일(日)요일]

2) Monday _____ [월(月)요일]

3) Tuesday _____ [화(火)요일]

4) Wednesday _____ [수(水)요일]

5) Thursday _____ [목(木)요일]

6) Friday _____ [금(金)요일]

7) Saturday _____ [토(土)요일]

Q. When is your birthday?   (너의) 생일이 언제야?
A. My birthday is October 24. (in 2002.)   10월 24일이야.
   It's March 31(st), 2010.   2010년 3월 31일.

(It's) March 31, 2010. 2010년 3월 31일.
(미식) 3. 31. 2010 (Mar. 31, '10)
(영식) 31. 3. 2010 (31 Mar. '10)

문장 쓰기 연습(1)

인생(삶의 정의) (Definition of life)

◆ (은유법, metaphor)

Life is a challenge. 인생은 도전이다.	— Meet it! 대응(응전)하라!
Life is a duty. 인생은 의무(임무)이다.	— Perform it! 이행(실행)하라!
Life is a goal. 인생은 목표가 있다.	— Achieve it! 성취(달성)하라.
Life is an opportunity. 인생은 기회다.	— take it! 찬스(chance)를 잡아라!
Life is a struggle. 인생은 투쟁(경쟁)이다.	— Fight it! (맞서) 싸워라!
Life is but a dream.	삶은 일장춘몽이다.

◆ (직유법, simile)

as busy as a bee.	꿀벌처럼 바쁘다.
as fat as a pig.	돼지처럼 비만(뚱뚱)하다.
as happy as a lark.	종달새처럼 행복하다.

문장 쓰기 연습(2)

인생의 소중한 가치(관) (Valuable point of view in life)

1) affection _____ [애정]

2) confidence _____ [신뢰. 자신감]
   cf. self-confidence

3) consideration _____ [배려. 고려]

4) cooperation _____ [협동(심). 협력]

5) courtesy _____ [예의. 예절]

6) effort _____ [노력]

7) enthusiasm _____ [열의. 열심]
   cf. passion (열정)

8) faithfulness _____ [충실성]
   cf. loyalty(충성심)

9) forgiveness _____ [용서]

10) freedom _____ [자유. 독립]
    cf. liverty(해방)

11) generosity _____ [관대함]

12) health _____ [건강]

13) honesty _____ [정직]

14) intelligence _____ [지성]

15) justice _____ [정의]
    cf. fairness (공평. 공명정대함)

문장 쓰기 연습(3)

인생의 중요한 가치 덕목(Most important worth in life)

1) love _____ [사랑]

2) modesty _____ [겸손. 사양]

3) responsibility _____ [책임감]

4) self- discipline _____ [자제(력)]
   cf. moderation (절제. 온건)

5) service _____ [봉사]

6) sympathy _____ [동정. 연민]

7) trust _____ [신뢰. 믿음]

8) thankfulness _____ [감사. 사은]
   cf. gratitude (사의. 감사한 마음). appreciation (사의)

9) understanding _____ [이해(심)]

10) wisdom _____ [지혜]

11) competence _____ [경쟁(력). 능력]

12) courage _____ [용기]
    cf. bravery (용감)

△ creativity (창의. 창조성). honor (명예). kindness (친절).
　patience (인내(심)) cf. tolerance 끈기 (관용).
□ conscience (양심). integrity (성실성) cf. sincerity (성실).

문장 쓰기 연습(4)

Poem(시)

Twinkle, twinkle little star

-Ann & Jane Tayler

Twinkle, twinkle little star;
How I wonder what you are
Up above the world so high
Like a diamond in the sky;
Twinkle, twinkle little star;
How I wonder what you are!

[반짝 반짝 작은 별]

_____

_____

_____

_____

_____

반짝 반짝 작은 별;
너는 도대체 무엇이냐?
세상 저 높이
하늘 위에서 다이아몬드처럼;
반짝 반짝 빛나는 작은 별;
너는 도대체 무엇이냐(궁금하다)?

영어펜맨십

발행일 · 2010년 9월 30일
발행인 · 우 제 군
발행처 · 예성출판사
저 자 · Brian Hwang
그 림 · 나하나
주 소 · 서울시 중구 을지로6가 18-55
TEL · (02) 2267-8739 · 2272-9646 · 2266-9153
FAX · (02) 2269-3393
등록일 · 1979. 11. 22
등록번호 · 제2-213

ISBN 978-89-7388-189-5

값 7,000원

※이 책의 내용을 무단으로 복사 · 전재할 수 없습니다.

문장 쓰기 연습(5)

Prayer(기도)

Dear God of us all.
We thank you for all the happiness of everyday.
We thank you for all the good things you give to us.
Help us (to) make other people happy, too.

-Amen

[기 도]

───────────────────────────────

───────────────────────────────

───────────────────────────────

───────────────────────────────

사랑하는 우리들의 하나님. 날마다 행복을,
선한 모든 것을 주신 것에 감사합니다.
또한 우리들로 하여금 다른 사람들도 행복하게 도와주소서.

발음 연습(Pronunciation Practice)

	B	V	F	P	L	R
1	ban	van	fan	pan	LAN	ran
2	base	vase	face	pace	lace	race
3	best	vest	fast	past	lest	rest
4	bine	vine	fine	pine	line	rime (rhyme)
5	robe	rove	fond	pond	cloth	cross
6	boat	vote	foul	pole	long	wrong
7	bury	very	fun	pun	lune	run

1) 금지. 반대하다 / 유개차 / 부채. 선풍기 / 냄비 / 지역방송(local area network) / run의 과거형
2) 기지. 기초/ 꽃병/ 얼굴 / 보폭. 속도 / 장식끈 / 인종. 경주(하다)
3) 최상의 / 조끼 / 빠른. 신속한 / 지난. 과거 / ~하지 않도록 / 휴식. 나머지
4) 덩굴 / 포도나무 / 좋은. 벌금 / 소나무. 갈망하다 / 선. 줄 / 운(율). 운이 맞다
5) 예복. 법복 / 헤매다. 유랑(하다) / 좋아하는. 다정한 / 못. 연못 / 천. 헝겊 / 십자가. 교차로
6) 작은 배 / 표결. 투표 / 더러운. 나쁜 / 막대기. 극지 / 긴. 오랜 / 나쁜. 틀린
7) 파묻다. 매장(하다) / 아주. 매우 / 재미. 즐거움 / 말장난. 익살 / 달. 반달모양 / 뛰다. 경영하다